WALKING
IN DARKNESS
THEN THE LIGHT

David M. Butler

To order additional copies of this book, contact:
Xlibris
844-714-8691
www.Xlibris.com
Orders@Xlibris.com

ISBN: Softcover   978-1-5434-9831-8
           EBook   978-1-5434-9832-5

Print information available on the last page

Rev. date: 09/13/2021

CONTENTS

INTRODUCTION

Drug addiction is an evil, despair filled circumstance and disease. Something that I didn't believe I would ever experience. Additionally, drug addiction is a destroyer of dreams as well as happiness. The first time I tried any drug I was instantly addicted even though I didn't realize it. My reality was denial and denial led me into a deep dark depression. Believing I was in control of my alcohol and marijuana addiction, I thought that trying harder drugs like cocaine, crack, meth and heroin wouldn't be a big deal. I have never been more controlled than under the influence of crack-cocaine. By the time I realized I was addicted to this powerful drug it was too late. The drug I thought I controlled now was controlling my every minute of every day. Even though it was affecting my health, occupation and relationships with the ones I loved here on Earth and Jesus in heaven, I couldn't stop. Nothing mattered to me anymore, and all I wanted to do was keep using. Little did I know how powerful crack was as well as other hard drugs were. The dark path I was walking for years grew darker and darker. The darkness that was pure evil brought me to the brink of death, and Satan wanted my soul. The following is a true story about my addiction to drugs, how they destroyed my life, and how the love of Jesus saved me from the hell I was living in.

Mathew 4: 16, "The people living in darkness have seen a great light, and those living in the land of the shadow of death a light has dawned."

Acts 9: 1-30, the story of Saul (St. Paul)

I would like to dedicate this book to my dad, Robert Butler, who passed away September of 2015, of Parkinson's disease. Also, to the addicted, depressed and anxious people of the world. Finally, to my cat Ophelia who was with me during my darkest times and my wife, Jennifer, that the Lord led me too after seeing his beautiful, bright light.

1

EL PASO

I moved to El Paso, Texas the summer of 1988 after graduating from the University of Northern Iowa. The Ysleta Independent School District recruited me to teach middle school math. Education was my major with an emphasis in math and science. I was looking to move somewhere south to get away from the cold of winter. El Paso is in the very southwest corner of the great state of Texas. The city sits on the borders of Mexico and New Mexico. Also, the city is located close to Phoenix, AZ where some friends of mine lived. Also, Ruidoso, NM was just a couple of hours northeast where it is mountain country and great snow skiing. I didn't know much about the city, but the weather was what I was looking for. Pretty much sunny and warm for most of the year.

Across the border of Mexico is the city of Juarez, MX. There are 2.5 million plus now, with El Paso included the area is over 3 million people. My first few years living in El Paso, I would go across the border to J-town (That is what you call Juarez living in El Paso) to party at the clubs. Young and dumb I didn't really think about the dangers of being in another country. Juarez is a city in MX that has a rough, tough and dangerous reputation. At that time the cartels didn't control J-town like they do now. The people of Mexico are wonderful people, but because of the cartels Mexico gets a bad rap. When we went to J-town it was to drink cheap tequila and cheap Mexican beer not for drugs, because get busted in MX you would probably never been seen again. Anyway, what ever drug I wanted I could get in El Paso.

My first year of teaching I stayed sober during the work day. Starting my second year of teaching I would get high before going to work. It wasn't long until I would take some with me and get high during the lunch time. I would drive to a park close to school or to a friends' house to get high before the afternoon classes. Honestly, I still didn't think I was addicted all I knew I liked smoking weed. I guess I was in denial, but all I knew there was no way I could ever get addicted to drugs, not me.

In college, I did coke a few times, but I didn't have the cash to buy a lot, so I would just do it at a party or when a bud had some. If someone offered I was all in because it can't be that bad. I can't become addicted I'm just having fun and can stop anytime I wanted. I did acid, shrooms and speed during college as well. Not my thing really those drugs didn't do it for me. There were some dudes that would do like ten tablets at a time, and they were basically zombies. I couldn't understand how they could do so much of that shit. Well, I guess they were addicted to it and would do it to the point of death. I almost died one night in college doing acid, I guess it was from a bad batch.

My cocaine use increased greatly the first couple of years in El Paso. It got to the point that I would do it every weekend, but not during the week until my last few years in west Texas. I found out how to freebase coke from some people, which is what addicts did before crack was on the streets. I heard about crack and how addictive it was, but my mentality was that I wasn't addicted to weed and coke, so I can handle crack.

There was no way that this hard drug was as dangerous as they said. The first time I tried crack I was instantly addicted to the powerful drug. I realized that I couldn't stop, so I was going to either die or be arrested, and I thought I would probably die. There was no way I'd be arrested because I felt I was too smart to be arrested.

2

MISERY

The depression that you feel once that drug is gone is utterly miserable. The anguish that you put yourself through is unbearable. Oh my God the anguish it gets so bad you just sob because of the despair and pane you feel. Also, the thoughts of suicide so the suffering would end.

To get over the anguish I would drink until I passed out. Anything not to think about the despair, I felt. What a rotten disease addiction is. I do hate it, it's mis-understood and I don't understand it myself. Addiction is the disease that leads to other diseases, i.e. lung, liver cancer etc. The crazy thing is that even though you're dying on the inside, you still, continue using drugs.

I thought I was going to die many times when I used cocaine and crack. Man, at least a couple hundred times, no fooling. I would do so much cocaine and crack pushing it to the limit that I thought my heart was going to explode. Also, I can't tell you how many times my nose would start bleeding. It was painful to the point that I would have to ice my nose, but when it felt better back to the snorting.

The last couple of years I lived in El Paso I was losing control because of my cocaine use. Probably and eight ball or two. My addiction grew to the point I would do some in my class room on my breaks. I knew that I could die anytime from my cocaine use, so I decided to sell everything including my house and move to the Phoenix area. I had some friends that had moved there after college, so needing a change I moved to Arizona. The summer of 2001 I moved to Tempe, Arizona just a few months before 9/11.

Tempe is the home of Arizona State, so the party scene was in full swing. I found a connection for weed after a few months living in the valley of the sun, but before that I suffered from not having any weed to smoke. Mainly anguish, frustration, and depression, so I was addicted to weed badly. I have heard some people say, "You can't get addicted to weed." I'm here to tell you I was addicted. I don't think it's as bad as cocaine and crack though. I craved cocaine, but had no clew where to get it, so I just drank and smoked weed my first year in the valley.

3

MEXICO

Before I moved to Tempe, in 2001, I went to Mazatlan, Mexico for a week with my girlfriend at the time. Awesome place, but so much poverty. The tourist area was really the only place to go. My first night when we were in Mazatlan we had dinner at a restaurant. Alicia had to go to the restroom at some point, and when she did that my time to talk with the waiter to see If he knew where to get some coke and smoke. Bingo, he showed me some powder and I tried it in the bathroom. It was pure stuff and more powerful than what I got in El Paso, so It was almost like a new and more intense high.

When I arrived in Tempe after my trip to Mazatlan, I looked for a teaching job, and got one with the Cartwright School District in Phoenix. The third city in Mexico that I visited was Puerto Vallarta. My, friend Eddie had been to the city a few times and on my fall break we went to Vallarta. Ed was an accountant, so he could make his own hours.

Wow! Puerto Vallarta what a beautiful city it is. Also, Ed had told me that the ratio of women to men was 7 to 1. Well, he was right, pretty much everywhere you looked another beautiful senorita. A funny story, the police in Mexico are a little shady, and one time walking back to the resort after partying I had to take a leak. I found a side road and started to pea when all of-a-sudden a 4 by 4 cop came rolling down the road. Oh, crap I knew there could be trouble. He rode over to me and I was busted. I was a bit scared because of the stories I heard about the Mexican police. He asked me what I was doing so I fessed up to it and told him followed by an apology. He told me to turn around, so I did, and he emptied my pockets. I only had like just $60 with me and, my, passport. When was done he put the passport and money back in, my, pocket. When I checked my cash a little while later I was about $40 short. We started laughing because I was just glad I didn't have go to jail. One could never be seen again if that would happen. The rest of the stay in Vallarta was great. The people are awesome. It's a great place to go on vacation.

When the school year was over I went to Vallarta during the month of June. During my stay there I met a sexy senorita at the zoo bar one night. She and her sister owned a condo at the Bay View Grand in the marina, a little north of the city. It was quite the resort. The pool was about a hundred meters long, or the length of a football field, broken into five sparkling sections. We hung out together for most of the vacation and kept in touch after I went back to Phoenix.

When I got back there was a problem with my Arizona certification. After fixing the problem I again taught at the Cartwright District but, I was assigned a different school. It was a bummer because I was teaching seventh grade science. It may first time teaching something other than math, and nice not having to worry about the math testing and the scores that had to be met. The new school was in a rougher part of the district and I was assigned to teach seventh grade math again. The math curriculum was not something I believed in, but I gave it a try.

It was a stressful time in my life because the mortgage company I sold my house through was scamming me. They owed me a second payment of six thousand dollars after the first year, but, were trying to get out of it. A girl I met in El Paso had a dad who was a lawyer, so they were going to handle my case but told me don't expect to win. When I heard that I lost hope in getting the money, so I got a little more depressed, and started doing cocaine again.

The curriculum turned out to be worse than I thought it was going to be, so after eight weeks I decided to leave my teaching position at fall break and flee to Mexico. Things weren't going great with the move to the valley, so I chose to run. I had gotten a hold of Maria, the girl I met back in June when I was in Vallarta. It turned out she was going to be there in October, so off I went to the beautiful Mexican resort destination once again. Back to the sun and drugs just what I needed to not think about the bad house deal. At least, that's what my mindset was.

4

HURRICANE KENNA

Hurricane season lasts until November 30, so there is always a chance that a hurricane could form off the pacific coast of southwest Mexico in October. That very thing then happened. The last week of October is when the hurricane hit. Growing up in a small town in Iowa there is not much of a chance witnessing a hurricane let alone a category 5 one. The days leading up to the hurricane making landfall it was a bit surreal. Beautiful sunny and warm days kicking it by the pool and looking at what seemed like diamonds sparkling in the ocean. As October 25 approached, the day Kenna was supposed to hit, it seemed more and more like a direct hit was in the future. Preparation grew more intense because Puerto Vallarta had never been hit by a hurricane for it was protected by the mountains. Until you witness one it seemed like a bit of a party atmosphere. So, there I was in Vallarta, upset because of the house issue, learning my dad had cancer of the prostrate and a category 5 hurricane was heading directly for us. The song, "Party like it's 1999" by Prince just came to my mind.

The days leading up to Kenna's arrival grew more intense with anticipation of what was about to happen but in, reality, none of us really had any idea on what was instore for us. Squalls were passing through that produced thunderstorm conditions, something I'm used to being from Iowa, the Hawkeye state. It all seemed pretty much normal to me so no big thing. The evening before Kenna hit, the storms brewing off the coast and over the mountains were becoming more ominous. It got so bad that the pirate cruise ship that took people on the dinner cruise had to stay in Banderas Bay.

The shit tried to go further out into the Pacific Ocean, but soon turned back to calm everyone's fears. The situation grew a bit tense.

When we arrived back to the condo, the first thing we did was turn on the TV to check out the latest news on Hurricane Kenna. I followed along as good as I could since my Spanish is more like Spanglish. Maria and her sister did the best to translate for me, so it was all good. It's always fun to check out another country's programming because it's a new learning experience. The station was showing a satellite picture of Kenna, it was a monster. It had the perfect eye wall and was about 150 miles southwest of Vallarta. There we were actually-watching a category 5 hurricane on satellite, like the one we've all seen on CNN, that was heading straight for us. As were watching with anticipation, all of-a-sudden, the screen turned to snow. We all looked at each other with amazement. That's when I realized that by the time morning came around, we we're going to witness something like we never had before.

When we woke up the next morning we immediately rushed for the siding glass door and looked over the balcony to see what was happening in the ocean. We were experiencing hurricane like conditions. The sky was grey, and the ocean was rumbling. The oceans surge was crashing through the tiki huts turning into broken pieces of drift wood. The ocean was rising, but the fifteen, foot sea wall was keeping the ocean off the property for the time being. At the full force of Kenna, the surge was so great that the ocean waves crashed over the sea wall and proceeded to fill the 100-yard long pool with 6 feet of sand. The ocean surge also brought the drift wood and sea boulders with it that resulted in the destruction of so of the first and second floor condos. Amidst all the destruction, it was fortunate for Puerto Vallarta that the eye hit about thirty miles north at Punto Gordo. If not, there would've been much more damage, although, it was extensive. The excitement and anticipation turned to despair and sorrow. A dreadful feeling came over me that I didn't want to experience something like that again.

The devastation at the Bay View Grand was only the beginning. The city of Puerto Vallarta sits behind the middle of Banderas Bay, nestled in the mountains. It is an utterly magical city filled with many shops like the silver jewelry stores and other indigenous souvenirs. The street heading into the city, Paseo Diaz Ordaz, was lined with large metal pristine sculptures depicting the Mexican culture. They were pretty much okay but not the downtown shops.

The city is protected by a sea wall as well. This one is about 30 feet high. It didn't have a chance against Kenna. The surge of the waves passed well over the wall crashing into the shops destroying the glass windows and taking the jewelry and other souvenirs back out with ocean to become part of it. The surge pushed into and up the city about 4 blocks. There was a pretty good, sized yacht washed up and parked three blocks up into the city.

Numerous homes and resorts along the coast were also damaged if not destroyed. Many of the locals had incredible stories of how the waves from the surge were at least ninety feet high rolling over La Playa de Los Muertos, the beach of the dead, and subsequently into the downtown shops. Looting did occur, but the Mexican military soon took care of that and restored order. You know you're in a different country when there are young men, probably in their late teen or early twenties, dressed in green military pants and white t-shirts riding around in the back of fully fledged large trucks, and armed with AK-47's.

5

STAY OR GO

The last couple of weeks with Maria were spent watching the Mexican laborers clean up the property, and checking out the clean up effort going on in the city. There's a lot of prejudice on both sides when it comes to Mexico, but if those people could have witnessed what I did, their walls of hatred just might have been penetrated. The temperature at that time of year in Vallarta is still in the upper eighties with humidity. Well, let me tell you these guys shoveled by hand approximately 45,000 cubic feet of sand in the hot, sweltering Vallarta sun. Keep in mind no machines were used just shovels and the laborer.

A couple of workers would start shoveling, continue to the point of collapsing, then hand the shovel to another guy while they would catch their breath and hydrate. This was a dawn to dusk project mind you, and after a week or so they hade a section of the pool ready for use again. The sections of the pool measured about 300 feet by 25 feet by 6 feet deep. Pretty hard work for 100 pesos per day, which was about $10 U.S. at the time.

Maria had rented out their condo for November to some tourists, so I had to make-a-decision, should I stay or go with her back to Cuenavaca where her mom lived. I decided to rent an apartment in the city and attempt to sell timeshares. I would have liked to go with her, but-in-reality, the drugs had a hold of me. I hoped that I could make some cash to help-out dad. He was a retired postman that drove a school bus to support him and mom. The kindest person I know and had great faith in Jesus.

The apartment that I rented was a studio on the second floor. It had a balcony with an ocean view, but, was about 3 blocks east of the coast. The rent was 2,300 pesos or $230 U.S. per month. There wasn't a whole lot to it, just a bed and bathroom with a shower. There was also a small fridge in the unit. You know what though it was great, just living in downtown Puerto Vallarta was awesome.

I landed a job at the Villa del Palmar selling time shares, and it was a resort that I had stayed at before. A three, star resort, and nothing like the Bay View Grand which was five stars. Like all the other resorts it took quite the beating from Kenna. The first and second floor villas were ravished by Kenna's force. Once again, a terrible sight to see. I would take the bus to and from work every day, stoned of course. The cost was 3 pesos each way or $0.60 U.S. round trip. The metro buses in Vallarta were old school buses painted white and blue. It was always an adventure taking the bus. Speeding down the road to your destination, as you're bouncing up and down because the shocks and streets haven't been repaired for years. Just as you are getting in the bouncing grove the bus would stop abruptly at a spot and drop off and pick up other hard, working souls. The transit system is very fast in Vallarta. If it was a city in the U.S., there would be multiple wrecks a day. If you live there you must be more careful because of the Federales, a word that makes everyone nervous. If they arrived, it was a large cash buy out or the car.

Working at a resort selling timeshares after a category 5 hurricane wasn't the choice I've ever made in hindsight. The thing was the drugs and hoped to make money. There were fewer tourists and more liner's. A, "Liner", is the one who takes you on the tour and presentation. They always say just ninety minutes, but we all know that's a bunch of poop. Me and Jenn were on one that dragged on for like four hours. When the dude slammed his pencil on the table I was done. I told him, "We are leaving now, or I will make the biggest scene in recent Vallarta history!", so he let us go and collect our items that we traded a life time for. I tried it for a couple of weeks, getting close a few times, but was ultimately let go because the lack of tourist's.

I decided to take the last two weeks off that I was going to live in Vallarta to enjoy the experience. My plane was due to go back to Phoenix in a couple of weeks, so let the party begin. I knew I would be back in Phoenix in a matter of weeks looking for a new teaching job. Dreading that thought, I had met a dude named Tory while working at the VDP and he was a partier as well. He was originally from Canada and moved there years ago. There are a lot of American's and Canadians living there that was surprising to me at the time. The first day off it was the beach, beer and weed during the day and a lot of cocaine, beer and weed at night. We made a good pair because he knew where to get drugs and I had the money and didn't really care.

6

THE FIRST TIME

The second week of constant partying I got what I wanted, crack. Tory knew a dude in one of the Cartel's named Jesus which is quite ironic. He had ordered another 8 ball and he threw in a gram of what turned out to be crack. We didn't have a stem, so we smoked it using a can. You'll use what ever is available when you're living in the addiction. About an hour later I think we got another gram of it and the crack addiction was on.

The first week we averaged probably an eight ball every couple of Nights and an ounce of weed a week at least, not to mention the booze. I guess you could say what the Eagles song messages you, "Living In the fast lane". A non-stop out of control binge the last two weeks there.

Tory was fluent in Spanish since he had lived there since he was a kid. We would walk the streets acting abhorrent and he would speak belligerently to the people as we looked for women and adventure. He almost got us in a couple of fights which isn't a good idea anywhere, but in Mexico if you get arrested you might not be seen for a while. Also, we were carrying drugs with us, not very smart. Thank you, Jesus.

I had dibble-dabbled with the stuff in the past, just enough to get a voracious appetite for the shit. It was an appetite acquired in El Paso when I would try to free base coke. It sucked because you would waste more coke than what you got turning it into the crack like substance you would get from the process. When we got the crack, I was excited because there was going to be enough to crave my appetite for it. Little did I know the addiction was just growing deeper in me.

The last week in Mexico I became more paranoid and isolated. We rarely went out any more. Only to get more beer, tequila, money and something to eat if anything at all. I just had to keep smoking crack and snorting cocaine never to be satisfied. Clubbing for girls turned into waving down taxis outside on the porch to go get some hookers for us. We were probably doing at least an eight ball of each at night. We would act belligerent on the balcony to people below and now and Then the Federales would cruise by an we would act the same way. They would leave us alone, but we walked the line just enough to be major assholes, however, I could tell they were hoping we would cross the line, so they could do their job.

It was a good thing the stay came to an end when it did, because I would have gotten in trouble or could have died I suppose. Leaving gave me a false sense of control over crack. I didn't know where to get it back in Phoenix, so I had to stop. The hunger stayed the same for the powerful hard drug. In the back of my mind I still had the convoluted hope that some day I would encounter the controlling drug that I thought I controlled, and oh boy, did I get me wish.

7

OPHELIA

I arrived back in Phoenix the second week of December one day. It had been two months since I had seen Ophelia, which had been the longest stretch of time I had been away from her since she blessed my life in 1993. I can remember walking into the house and seeing the little calico cat trotting towards me. She had a white underbelly and face with patches of orange, brown and black. I picked her up, gave her a big kiss and hugged her so hard, If, she was a balloon she would have popped.

Squeaky O was a special kitty. Her many talents were fetching rubber bands, rolling when directed to and answering back with a squeaky meow. Her "Meow" would change with the question asked and what mood she was in. Fifi was my little girl. It seemed as if there was a little person in there. To this very day, when I think about her doing her tricks it brings a smile to my eye and a tear rolling down my cheek. Ophelia died in 2007, but probably would have lived longer if it wasn't for my addiction to drugs. An addiction so intense that not even my love for her could penetrate it.

Ophelia stayed with a friend and former colleague of mine while I was in Vallarta. When I arrived back in Phoenix, Ray let Ophelia and I stay with his family and him while I looked for a mid-year teaching position. Ray is a good, old soul. Another teacher dedicating his life to help children and society. That year, there were no teaching positions at mid-year, at least not the districts I was concentrating on. Since there were no teaching jobs to speak of, I decided to give selling home security systems a try at a local home security firm for the month of January. I made enough money during the month, so I decided to get an apartment of my own. The apartment was at another seedy place in west Phoenix. Once again, not the best place to live but the rent was cheap. Walking and knocking, going door to door 6 days a week wasn't my thing after all, so I decided to leave the home security system business after January. For the months of February and March, I decided to take some time off, spend some time with Ophelia, before looking for a substitute teaching position for the last 2 months of the school year. My drug use continues, and once again the drugs I used were marijuana and cocaine. There were a couple of crack-addicted prostitutes that would come around from time to time, but I never pursued the drug remembering the last tow out of control weeks in Vallarta. I resisted the temptation for the time being.

I landed a substitute teaching job with the Mesa Public Schools for the last two months of the 2002-2003 school year. The money wasn't great, but it was fun teaching at the elementary level, especially after teaching at the middle school level for over fourteen years. Don't get me wrong, I love the middle school child and I got into teaching at that level because of my own struggles when I was in seventh grade. But it's a beast you can't understand unless you've experienced it. I really feel that everyone should teach a week at some level, then you'd understand the sacrifices teachers make for the parents' children. You may think that teaching is easy, but it is one of the hardest things I've ever done. We teach for the love of the children, because it's certainly not for the money.

At the end of the school year, Ophelia and I went back to Iowa for a month or so to spend time with my family. It was also my 20 year high school reunion. I didn't know where to get drugs in the metropolis know as Waukon, Iowa, so I took a quarter pound of week with me for my own personal use. It was good seeing a lot of old friends that I hadn't seen for many years, but my drug use was still controlling me.

No one knew I was smoking pot, because I kept it very well hidden. In college I wrote a paper about marijuana use and learned that one can adapt to smoking weed and everyday life. I got high when I woke up and was high when I went to bed at night, something I had been doing since 1989. It definitely wears you down, but not as much as using hard drugs like heroin, meth, cocaine and crack.

Ophelia and I left Iowa sometime in July and on the way back we had a close call with a tornado. I had checked the forecast the night before we left, and, like many summer days in the mid-west, there as a chance for severe weather the following day. The drive through Iowa and Nebraska was uneventful, so I figured there was no chance to see a tornado. Tornadoes are phenomena I've been fascinated with since I was a child. Well, as we left Nebraska and traveled into Colorado on I-76, the clouds were becoming more, dark. As we passed Sterling, CO the clouds were quite ominous rolling off the Rocky Mountains. It turns out that I was looking at a horizontal funnel cloud. Before I knew it, it was black as night even though it was only mid-afternoon. There were grass and dirt flying through the air as we continued down the interstate. I could feel the force of the tornado pulling the truck when I realized we were only going about 35 mph even though the pedal was to the metal. I was thinking about pulling over and getting Ophelia with me into the ditch next to the road, but then I saw a, "Next Exit ½ Mile" sign. We made it to the exit. I was going to pull under the over pass, but it was filled with cars. I took a little dirt road to a convenience store that was full of gas pumps and propane tanks. As I was turning the truck around to position u in a better spot to leave if things got worse, I saw what looked to be an F-5 tornado rolling across the field on the other side of the interstate. It was a huge, black monster and luckily it was approximately 5 miles away from us. After the tornado lifted, I decided to hit the road again since we were parked in dangerous area. We took off and after 15 minutes or so of erratic, frantic driving the front passed and the sun brightened the skies again.

After camping a couple of days in the beautiful Colorado wilderness, Ophelia and I headed back to Phoenix. My friend Ray, who I mentioned earlier, was kind enough to put us up again for a week or so as I looked for a teaching position for coming 2003-2004 school year. I received calls from different districts, but I was holding out for Mesa Public Schools. I got the call in mid-July from Mesa and it turned out they had numerous math openings at different schools. Ultimately, I settled on teaching eighth grade math at Shepherd Junior High. I had always wanted to teach in that district. It was something about teaching in one of the largest districts in Arizona, and the pay would be a bit more, too. Up to this point, I had taught in districts that had middle schools and utilized the middle school philosophy, but Mesa's were junior high schools. Junior highs are a bit like small high school factors. I knew it would be an adjustment, but I was willing to give it a shot. A little more money is huge for a teacher, especially when that teacher is an addict.

My appetite for cocaine dwindled because I had done so much of it in the past. I would do so much, that my nose would bleed. Despite that, I would just keep on snorting the drug. Just the smell of cocaine made me sick. I can't tell you how many times I thought I was going drop dead as my heart pounded and I couldn't catch my breath. I was still smoking marijuana every day, despite that the first year at Shepherd JH was a successful one. My students test scores were solid and I coached the 9th grade boys tennis team to a city championship. It was the first boys' tennis championship in school history, so it was cool to be a part of. Those kids were very talented. If we hadn't won, the championship it would have been a disappointing year. Those kids hold a special place in my heart to this day, and I hope they are doing well and drug free. The banner that we won, and the banner that I won't ever see again, is hanging from the rafters in the gym. The reason I won't ever see it again is that I've been banned from the Mesa schools' property for life because of what happened the next year. Just another thing that drug addiction had deprived me of.

The school year ended the last week of May, so for the month of June I headed back down to Puerto Vallarta. My addiction to crack cocaine and I were hoping to find Cory, so we could continue what had started back in 2002. After looking a few days for him, I had no luck. Just a few people said that they may have seen him here or there, but no good leads. Since Cory wasn't available, I had to get the drugs I craved to feed my addiction from my old sources. One night when I was hanging out at the Zoo Bar, I met a couple of real good people. His name was Manny and hers was Dawn. They were closers at a timeshare resort in Nuevo Vallarta, a tourist area about 10 miles north of Puerto Vallarta. A closer is someone that finalizes the timeshare deal. There were transplanted Canadians and they liked to party.

We hung out the last couple of weeks and there was plenty of coke and smoke. Even though the smell of cocaine made me sick, I still did it because I was an addict, it was available, and crack cocaine wasn't. It was also the first time that I did ecstasy. I have to say I liked it. It apparently has a bit of heroin in it, so I can see how it would be very addictive and has destroyed many lives. Heroin and ecstasy were two drugs that weren't available to me during my drug years, Or I would have become addicted to them as well. I know heroin would've been the end of me after hearing some of the horror stories about it. Manny wanted me to stay down there and work at the timeshare, but ironically, I didn't want to keep doing cocaine. Since I was under contract to teach for Mesa schools for the 2004-2005 school year, ultimately, I went back to Arizona. That's when my personal addiction-from-hell story erupted.

8

THE BEGINNING OF THE END

I arrived back in Mesa the first week of July, and, moved into the hotel turned into apartments. It turned out it was the worst decision of my life. I started moving my things into the apartment on warm Mesa evening, and that's when I met the devil himself who went by the name of Jack. Jack was a crack-head that preyed on other, people's addiction to fuel his own. I can remember seeing him leaning up against the balcony of the second floor and telling myself that this guy looks like trouble. I turned out he was. As I was carrying a load up to the apartment, he acknowledged me and I him. You know small talk like, "Hey how are you doing dude?" "Good, how about you?" Stuff like that. He was a likeable guy, he had the gift of gab. Now, I realize he was a predator preying on someone's addiction to buy him drugs and fuel his addiction. Me and my addiction to crack was his meal ticket. After moving my stuff into the apartment, I bought some beer and invited him over for a cold one. Of course, Ophelia came trotting out of the room to entertain the new guest. He, like all others that met the fuzzy little feline, was captivated and charmed. She wooed even those that didn't like cats.

She went right over to Jack and started rubbing against his legs walking back and forth in front of him. Ophelia would always meander over to a guest like that bringing a smile to their faces. Jack was quite amazed that a precious, little, delicate creature like her could show him any affection. Probably something to do with growing up in the environment he did. It turned out he was and ex-gang member from Los Angeles. I know cats rub against people to transfer their scents to them, but it truly seemed like there was a little person inside Ophelia. It was then that Jack uttered those infamous words as he said, "Could I borrow some money from you, so I can get some medicine?" I knew it must be for some illegal drug, and it turned out to be for crack. I gave him $20 and said there was only one condition, that I could smoke some too. It was another terrible choice that I had made in a matter of hours.

Sitting on pins and needles for an hour or two in anticipation, he finally came back with the hard drug that I craved so much since becoming addicted in '02 when I lived in Vallarta. To smoke crack in Mexico we use a can because we didn't know where to get a glass pipe and anyway we were to paranoid to go look anyway. This was the first time I used a glass pipe to some crack. It was a much purer hit so more powerful than what I had experienced in the past. It felt like my addiction grew more intense and to a new level. I immediately was asking for more, it was just what Jack was hoping would happen. I drove him to the crack house that he had gotten the first rock, so we could get another $20.

The place we drove to was, a sleazy part of the city. The hotels were sleazy as well. The tenants were basically drug dealers and used to turn tricks. More enfeebled than where I lived even. The apartments made my place seem like something that is wasn't. Jack directed me where to go, then we pulled up to a room. He got out of the truck and I waited for him there. There is nothing more nerve racking than waiting outside a crack establishment and having the cops cruise by. It knew it was foolish and wrong, but when you're addicted it doesn't even matter anymore. Apathy makes consequences a mute, point.

This was going to just a one, night stand with the beige colored drug, but Jack and my addiction had different thoughts. There was still a month before school was going to start so, I felt like no problem I'll stop before the start of the new year. I was wrong, because when I woke up the next morning, which was probably the last good night of sleep I had the next nine months, because my addiction wanted more crack, etc. I kept telling myself that I just needed to stop before the start of school, and everything would be alright, so with that pep talk I once again knocked on the devil's door ready to get more. The $20 amount became $40 and I was starting to realize that I couldn't stop smoking crack. It was a different feeling from other drugs I did. I mean I would stop other drugs in the past because, I wanted to take a break and be sober. Not this shit I just had to smoke even though I wanted to stop. My addiction blew up in face and I didn't know what to do. The tan I brought home from Vallarta was turning pale.

August was here, so I knew now I had to stop because the school year was starting in a few days. I formed a terrible habit the last month. Research shows that doing something everyday for three and a half weeks a habit is formed. That habit could be good or bad depending on what you are doing. Since, I smoked crack for a month straight or so I would have to quit the crack for at least three and a half weeks to form the habit of not smoking. Much easier said then done because, I couldn't stop, and I started to get worried. Especially hard with a crack-head living next door. Needless-to-say, instead of quitting, my addiction progressed and I was losing control.

The first week of school started the first week in August, like around the fifth. The first five days consisted of boring meetings, learning, strategies, and concepts that were learned previous years, that's the government for you. Not a practical use of time like setting up the class room, so the children would have the best first day that leads to a good year. Not a practical way to use precious time, but that is how the GOV, rolls. It was always hard starting the new year after the summer, but, being addicted to crack was deathly difficult.

The five days of meeting were usually separated by the weekend to ease the teachers into the new year. I prayed on my knees that those five days would finally crave the crave I had, so I would be ready to teach the children crack free. After the meeting was over on the first Thursday I made up an excuse, so I could leave and start smoking that deadly drug crack.

It was the last weekend before the students started on the next Thursday. Instead of stopping smoking crack I gave in to my addiction and we probably smoked two eight balls, which is about seven grams. Not getting any sleep that weekend Monday morning came around way to soon, and it was time for another three days of stupid meetings. Reality was setting in and in four days the students would be back, and I was addicted to crack-cocaine.

Smoking at least a gram a night, so not getting any sleep I started the Year off pretty much a zombie. Thursday and Friday, the first two days, went well. It is mostly paperwork, handing out supplies, and getting to know the children. When the day ended on Friday I couldn't get out of there fast enough to smoke more crack. We smoked at least an eight ball that weekend and ended up getting a few hours of sleep. I could tell the second, hand smoke was affecting Ophelia, but I couldn't stop, I'd tell myself that I was killing her, but I was too far gone. Not sleeping the entire weekend, I took Monday off. It was just the third day of school and the first time in fifteen years I took a day off the first week of the school year. The new tennis season was starting soon, so, it would be another three hours later in the day until I could smoke crack again. Instead of sleeping the madness continued, and we smoked another gram Monday.

Somehow, I made it to work Tuesday and made up some lame excuse why I called in sick Monday. I had people fooled at that point because there was no way they knew about my addiction. The secretary asked me if I was losing weight since I wasn't eating, and, looked a bit skinny. I had always worked out by lifting weights and doing cardio, but when I got addicted to cocaine and crack that ended. Smoking a gram of crack at night and not sleeping made teaching very difficult, but I had a job to do, so I did the best I could.

As September arrived I was getting more worried because my addiction was running ramped.

I was getting more and more worried because I was starting to realize I Couldn't quit smoking. A feeling I didn't have with other drugs, well cocaine for a while when I was living that hell as well. In mid September the Hawkeyes were playing a game at Sun Devil Stadium. Growing up in Iowa I am a huge Hawkeye fan, Go Hawks! The Friday Before the Saturday game the I-club was holding a rally at a sports bar In Tempe. I was supposed to meet my good friend John of 30 years to celebrate the weekend game that evening. I couldn't stop smoking crack, and I missed the rally. John and I only had sisters, so we were like brothers. We also roomed together at Northern Iowa, Go Panthers! There is only one thing that would make me miss a party for the Hawks with a great friend. That thing was crack-cocaine and the addiction that shadows it. I felt terrible, but I was so addicted I couldn't stop.

Jack and I stayed up all night once again smoking crack and, the next day the Hawks were playing ASU. John didn't know I was smoking crack because, I was ashamed that I was smoking the illegal drug and I was still able to handle okay. I was in denial and just knew for sure that there was no way I could be addicted to crack. There was a pre-game party Saturday at 1pm, in Tempe, to get ready for the game later that evening. John picked me up a little before 1pm and off we went to drink and cheer on the Hawks. I wasn't easy putting down the crack pipe, but the Hawks were in town, and I wasn't going to let John down again. I immediately started drinking heavily to stop the yearning for crack. By the time the game started I was quite intoxicated. We had nose bleed seats in the Iowa section at Sun Devil Stadium. The game did not go very well for Iowa and I became quite belligerent. I don't remember what the score was half way through the second quarter, but it was a blow out, and the game was basically over. I started screaming obscenities to the football team and the Iowa fans didn't like what they were hearing, and we were kicked out of the game. Pretty embarrassing, but I was almost glad for I could smoke more crack again with in the hour, so sad.

September ended the way it had started, constantly smoking crack, hardly eating and not sleeping for days at a time. Realizing that I couldn't stop was real scary. I didn't seek help because of the shame I felt, and I didn't want to burden anyone with my problem. I got myself Into, this mess, and I'll get myself out of it. I knew my teaching was suffering and I felt terrible about that, so I just did the best I could living with a horrific addiction.

9

LOSING CONTROL

When October arrived, I had more time on my hands because tennis was finishing up. I was able to leave school at 4 pm now compared to 5:30 pm when I was coaching. I would smoke for longer amounts of time, so I was smoking more crack-cocaine. My addiction went to yet another level. At this point, I was spending 60% or more of my pay check each month on crack. For the next two weeks, I slept maybe twelve hours the whole time. I had been telling myself the last three months that I would get bored with the hard drug and quit. I couldn't! Again, when you feel like you're in control, and then realize you're not it is quite horrifying. Anyone who thinks they can control drug use is a fool and only kidding themselves. That is exactly what I was, a fool.

In mid-October we had a fall break. Early release on Wednesday for the students, but I was able to skip out early. John and I had scheduled a trip to Las Vegas like we did each Fall. I was supposed to leave Thursday morning. John was going to meet me there Saturday. Before that though, when I raced home Wednesday afternoon Jack and I once again left for the crack den. We smoked all night once again and I ended up missing my flight on Thursday. The reason was I was a convict to this drug, crack. We ended up smoking all night not getting any sleep again. I made it to the airport on Friday morning having enough time left to find a bar. When I found one I sat at the bar area and got a large draft, and a shot of tequila. After I got my wits together I noticed a hot, blonde business woman sitting next to me. We hit it off and talked and drank for the hour and a half before we boarded our flights. During the conversation it turned out she was flying to Reno, but, had a connecting flight in Vegas. We went our separate ways and when I got on the flight I looked to the left and she was sitting next to the window with the other seat open. I asked if I could sit with her so-we, snuggled as we flew to Vegas.

The topic of drugs came up at some point, and I told her about what was happening with me and the addiction to crack. It turned out she was from Las Angeles, and, moved to Reno to get away from all the drugs be it heroin, meth, cocaine and crack. I asked her to stay over night in Vegas with me, but, her schedule dictated the outcome. It wasn't meant to be and leaving the plane was difficult as we looked at each other and knew we would never see each other again. Anyway, When I got to the casino I slept the whole day because the exhaustion I felt was really getting critical.

The trip was a bummer since I was dealing with my withdrawals from crack and other drugs, illegal or legal. I felt bad because I let my best friend down. We always had a great time just drinking, gambling and staring at the big screens watching the next football game. When Sunday came it was betting on games until it was time to make the flight to Phoenix.

When I got back to the apartment I made sure Squeaks Ophelia was doing well. After the sight of my precious sweetheart resting, I still knocked on Jacks door and we went for some more shit. After a weekend of drinking in Vegas and then smoking the crack Sunday night, I made it to school the next day, but not the best I've been. I was a bit out of it drunk and tweaking.

There were five more weeks until Thanksgiving break. To tell you the truth I didn't think I would make it to then, and actually-hoped I wouldn't, but I did.

Finally, the holiday arrived and not a minute to soon. My body was becoming run down due to the constant crack-smoking and getting no sleep. I was five months into a crack addiction where I averaged around eight hours of sleep a week. Exhausted, I still made to school and did the best I could. Some friends and co-workers were starting to notice that I was losing weight. There were a couple of friends that asked me if I was smoking crack, but I just denied it and said I was fine. The shame you feel during an addiction is overwhelming. I didn't want to burden anyone with my problem. I got myself addicted to crack and into this mess, so I was going to get myself out of it some way or die trying.

Even though I didn't want to keep using my addiction progressed to two grams a day. I don't think I slept the entire brake before school started again on Monday. I could tell that the smoke was getting to Ophelia and affecting here more and more. At times I would wipe tears from her eyes and then wipe the tears from my eyes as well. I was killing this special little fuzz ball of a cat who felt like a part of me. My biggest fear was dying of an overdose and leaving her alone in this cruel world. The disease of addiction could give a rat's ass about love, because addictions main focus is misery and death.

A December arrived I knew I was in trouble. Not fully understanding addiction, I didn't understand why I couldn't stop and put down the crack pipe. The despair I felt from the addiction was utterly terrible. I felt like I was probably going to end up dying from my drug use now. Even though I felt this way I didn't ask for help because I thought it was a sign of weakness, but now I know that asking for help is a sign of strength.

My niece's birthday is on December 3rd, so feeling like each day could be my last I called Amelia the night before to wish her a happy birthday. My sister thought this was so kind, but in reality, I wasn't sure I'd be alive on the 3rd. Then a few days later I got in touch with a former girlfriend in El Paso who had been working on a real estate deal that went sideways. I had lost touch with her due to addiction and feeling hopeless. She informed me that we had won the case, but since I was no where to be found the judgement was lost. This news drove me deeper into addiction and the apathy I felt grew stronger and my will to live was fading.

Finally, Christmas break was here and maybe I could some how break the chains that held me captive. I was hoping to sleep, eat and get healthy, but that didn't happen. The strangle hold that the crack addiction had on me was too strong. I ended up smoking and drinking the break away. I had been asking my Lord and Savior, Jesus the Christ for help to stop for a few months now, and he was starting to give me some signs that trouble was growing near. i.e. the first weekend of break Jack and I went to the crack infested area of Mesa that we had been going to, to score. When we got to the place he jumped out of the truck and ran in to get a gram or two of the terrible hard-drug. He came back empty handed, his dealer told him that the area was hot and there were rumors that a bust could take place. We sped out of there and went across the street to a fast food place so we could check things out. Well, all of a sudden there were eight or so cars screaming up to the place. A bunch of undercover cops jumped out of the cars and with guns drawn, raided the place we were just at. It was like an episode of "The Shield", the cop show from the early to mid-2000's.

It was quite surreal, and I just sat there in the truck mystified from what I was seeing. That was the first real sign from the almighty God to quit or else. The thing is I was so addicted to crack all I wanted to do was keep smoking that crap.

After reality sat in, instead of being relieved, we were bummed because we didn't have any crack to smoke. After freaking a bit Jesse remembered an old connection, so off we went on another chase. This dude's name was Louis and he was living in the same general area so off we went. Once again, this guy lived in a hotel you could rent by the week. I was getting tired of supporting Jesse's habit, so after a couple of scores I started to go by myself to the place. I was smoking close to two grams a day during the break and when I didn't think it could get any worse, it did. A few days before Christmas I got a call from my mom and by the tone of her voice I knew it wasn't good. My cousin T, a great young man had just graduated from college that semester. He and a friend went to a Christmas party an hour or so away from where he lived with my Aunt and Uncle. They decided to leave later that night and on there way home the car hit some black ice then they lost control of the car and crashed. T was ejected and killed, but his friend lived. After mom told me I lost it. I couldn't believe what I was hearing! Here I was addicted to crack-cocaine and felt as if anyone deserved to die it was me not my younger cousin. I was floored and fell deeper into darkness. I felt responsible in a way and really started to hate myself.

Addiction makes one very selfish, and that is why I started going over to Louis' crib on my own, so I could smoke all the crack myself. It didn't take him long to start taking advantage of me also. For instance, I would pay for an eight ball and get maybe a third of that. I knew I was getting ripped off but didn't care because I was so far gone. Addiction really makes no sense, it is truly a disease and mental health issue.

On January 1st the Hawkeyes were playing LSU in the Capital One Bowl. John had invited me over to watch the game with him and his family. Christmas break was coming to an end and I'm sure I had slept even ten hours leading up to game time. Kick-off was at 11:30, so I had to make it. I made it just in time for the start of the game even though it was a struggle. I felt terrible, but at half I made an excuse to go home so I could get high. I made it back after the second half started, so I felt even worse. During the fourth quarter I started slipping in and out of consciousness. It was a great game that went right down to the end. I snapped to just in time and there were probably thirty seconds left in the game and LSU had just scored to take the lead. The Hawks got the ball and drove down the field as time was running out. The clock management wasn't very good like always and at about ten seconds left there was utter chaos. We were all yelling at the TV for them to call a time out. The Hawks hurried to the line and as LSU was the team in chaos, Tate threw a long touchdown pass as time ran out. I almost missed that historic play because of crack. I made a lame excuse, so instead of spending the day with him and his family watching bowl games like usual I left and sped back home to the crack pipe and the hell I was living.

10

EMINENT DEATH TO LIFE

January 3rd was the first day of the second semester. I started the semester exhausted from a six-month crack addiction. I slept just a handful of hours the previous two and a half weeks of Christmas break. I literally had one foot in the grave. To make things worse I soon found out that the administration was taking two of my best classes away, and, replace them with two classes of unruly students. Many of the students had behavioral problems. To deal with the new, found stress I started leaving school during my breaks to smoke crack. I was spinning out of control.

One day after school I called Louis for another gram, but his phone was disconnected. I went to the Tempe apartment anyway to see if he was there. It turned out he moved out, so my source was gone. The previous couple of times there I noticed a couple of shady characters hanging around. They were there once again, so since dude split I asked them if they knew where to get some crack. They went into one of the apartments, and after a few minutes they came back out to invite me in. They introduced me to a young woman who went by the name of "Giggles". She asked me what I was looking for and I replied, "Crack-cocaine." She gave me an actual gram for $40, so I was quite happy. I sped back to my apartment to smoke not knowing that this was the beginning of the end.

The rest of January I was spiraling more and more out of control. I was heading for a huge crash. Constantly smoking crack before, during and after school plus getting no sleep at night was slowly killing me. It was becoming apparent that something was wrong and people were starting to notice. A friend of mine, Tony, was questioning me if I was smoking crack, but I just denied it because the addiction was so enticing. Tony and his girl Kate would invite me over to grill out and if made it I would be at least an hour late. The crack pipe wouldn't let me go.

By the time February came around I was in bad shape. I was strung out and dying as a result of the seven-month addiction to crack. There were times in class that I would almost fall asleep and fall to the floor.

John and I went to the Phoenix Open golf tournament which is something we would always do. As we were sitting by one of the greens I laid back and immediately fell asleep. Also, I was extremely hungry since I hadn't been eating much. That's another thing with smoking crack and doing cocaine you just don't eat. We got a hot dog at some point from one of the venders and I gobbled it down. It was the only thing I ate the last two days. I could tell John knew something was up since I passed out and devoured a hot dog. I just fibbed so he wouldn't worry about me.

The following Sunday was the Super Bowl which was on February 6th in 2005. I went to another friends' house for a SB party, and somehow, I made it. Friends Mark, Candice and Janet organized a surprise birthday party for me as well since I was turning 40 the next day which was February 7th. They were awesome and very thoughtful to do that for me. Whoever first said that life begins at forty was a very wise person.

I ended up taking Monday off since it was my birthday. Really it was just another excuse to waste another day smoking crack. SJH has a cake for teacher's when it's their birthday. Not showing up and all the erratic behavior I had been displaying the principal decided to put me under investigation.

The last three weeks of February were a nightmare. I'm not sure if I slept at all those days. Smoking non-stop, not eating and not getting any sleep was taking its toll. I came close to passing out in class when I would be sitting at the overhead projector and doing math problems. One day after school when I was speeding home, I almost didn't notice a line of cars at a red light. I noticed the cars at the last second and slammed on the breaks stopping just in time. Praise to God because I would have killed someone for sure. At night I would weep and beg God to help me stop. I could tell Ophelia was becoming more ill as well from the second-hand smoke. It was a horrifying circumstance.

I was receiving numerous signs from the Lord, but I was too far gone and didn't care anymore. My behavior was becoming more and more disturbing as well. I'm pretty sure the Mesa PD had my apartment under surveillance because I could hear people talking below my back window. I lived on the second floor, and the cops would congregate in the back, parking lot. I would blow the smoke out of the window to try to keep it from Ophelia. There were times that there would be a flash outside, so I guess they were trying to get photo evidence. I made it into a bit of a game and put on all black like a ninja so it would be harder to see me. The addiction was making me insane it seemed like.

From weeping as I prayed to the Father to help me stop, to taking another hit blowing smoke out the window slowly killing myself and Ophelia. One night I drove to a convenience store down the road to get some beer to counteract the crack high, and a cop pulled me over. I hadn't been drinking yet so there was no alcohol on my breath, so he let me go after I passed a quick sobriety test. If that wasn't a sign I don't know what was, but I had accepted that there was no hope and it my time to die. That is what addiction does, it takes all hope away from its victims.

After school on February 28th I rushed to Giggles house and scored a couple of grams. I was up all-night smoking again and ran out of the illegal drug at about 5am on March 1, 2005.

I drug myself to school and got through my first period class. When the bell rang at 10am I hit the road for Giggles to score another gram. Ten minutes later I at the crack den. Quickly I went inside and got another gram of the drug. As I was walking out the door to my truck I noticed a helicopter hovering overhead. I wondered if that was because of me, but, shrugged it off and hit the road for my apartment. I raced home since I didn't have a lot of time before my next class. I was feeling a bit nervous because of the helicopter that I had noticed at Giggles. I checked the truck mirrors to see if anyone was following me, but, didn't notice anyone behind me so I thought everything was okay. As I pulled up to my complex I noticed a police cruiser facing me. He stopped and waited for me to pull in the parking lot and that's when he lit me up with the cherries. I noticed an unmarked car came zooming into the lot and I knew it was over. I parked the truck, got out and waited for the undercover officers to come over and make the arrest. As I waited at least another six unmarked cars came rolling into the parking lot. It was kind of like the scene I witnessed across from the fast food joint as we watched the raid on the crack house weeks earlier. I actually had time to run or somehow get rid of the rock, but I just stood there. I was actually thankful it was over. When a number of cops came upon me I raised my arms and said it was in my pocket. After the cop got the gram of crack out of my pocket he said, "You know this is our stuff, don't you?" Saying those words with a sly smile as he looked at me I said, "No I don't I'm just glad it's over." I truly believe I would have been dead by the end of the month if I wasn't arrested, so I guess they saved my life. Nobody at Shepard Junior High ever approached me to asked if there was anything wrong. That would have nice if someone did, but I would have probably lied and denied it.

I checked myself into rehab about a week later at Banner Health Rehabilitation Center. I lived at 12-step program meeting the next few months before my case came up. The program kept me clean and gave me hope. Sometime in July my time to see the judge came. Going to rehab on my own and staying clean was good for me and I was able to take a plea deal. I was placed on probation for a year and a half. If I completed the program then I would avoid prison and be convicted of a misdemeanor instead of a felony. It wasn't easy, but I served out my term successfully and was discharged. I was free once again! All glory to Jesus.

11

FREEDOM

After successfully completing probation I was free late June of 2006. Regaining my freedom came at a cost though. The sum of lawyer fees, fines and all the other expenses that the system nickels and dimes you to death was more than $10,000. Also, I spent a small fortune on crack the eight months I was addicted to it. The last couple of months I probably spent about $2,000 per month. So, the total price was well over $20,000 from summer 2004 to the summer of 2006. That was just the monetary price.

It was a blessing that the state of Arizona passed a law just a handful of years before my arrest back in 2005. The law allowed first time offenders to rehabilitate themselves by serving probation. Now, if you screw up probation then off to prison you would go. God gave me the strength to stay clean, sober and out of trouble during my stint on probation. Thankyou Jesus.

Gaining back my freedom, that I had taken for granted, meant I could leave the state of Arizona for the first time in two years. In 1998 I bought a timeshare. Yes, I got fooled also. If you do make the decision to fall into that trap, you've got to use it or It makes no sense at all. You would just be throwing money away like you do when you smoke crack.

Being able to get a condo in Kauai, HI in September was possible, so I decided to take a trip to paradise since I had just lived and survived hell on Earth. I had been there in 1990 with some friends who had a, wait for it, a timeshare, so I knew the Island a little bit. Kauai, "The garden island", got its name because of the lush and colorful landscape. The shades of green are amazing. It was actually a bit ironic being there because what the previous two years were like. My good friend Kookie took care of Ophelia for me while I was away.

Kauai was more beautiful than I remembered. Probably because I had a clear head that visit. When I was there in 1990 I had been addicted to weed for about six years and cocaine for about three years. And yes, I found some Hawaiian sweet leaf back then. I knew I could get it this trip too. Actually, there was a guy when I got close to the resort on the side of the road and I knew he had some. He was waving people over to him for crying out loud. It crossed my mind, but I was still anxious because what had happened the last two years, so I didn't go there. The trauma you experience during an addiction like that is horrifying.

I'm pretty sure I have PTSD because I have nightmares all the time.

The trip was quite lonely because the way I felt after living through what I did. I didn't have a great opinion of myself so I punished myself with isolation. I was a bit down, but in Hawaii and freedom was mine again. I drank beer, went to the beautiful beaches and watched football. I just wanted to be alone. One day I went boogie boarding at a beach whose tempestuous reputation proceeded it. As I was floating in the turbulent ocean I got caught in a rip tide. It's a scary thing if it has ever happened to you. I panicked and starting splashing helplessly trying to get out of the tide. I became exhausted and was starting to lose the battle. As the waves continued crashing over my head I was gulping down salt water, I was drowning. I thought to myself that if I was going to die it might as well be in paradise. A peaceful feeling came over me and then it felt like someone was pushing me from behind my back and before I knew I could touch the bottom and keep my head above the salty water. As I made my way to the beach I looked around to see if there was anyone, but there was no one in sight. I finally dragged myself to the sand and collapsed. I know now it was the hand God that pushed me to shore. It wasn't my time to leave planet Earth yet.

12
FAMILY

When I got back from Kauai, I knew I had to see my family back in the Midwest. Narrowly escaping death once again, I felt my chances were running out. Since my crack addiction and subsequent arrest, I had not seen them for about three years. My dad had been diagnosed with prostrate cancer a year earlier. I felt terrible not being around the last few years but being addicted to weed and coke took me away from them years before.

I've always been a bit shy. I guess it's low self-esteem. After the arrest it hit a new low. Thanksgiving was coming, so I decided to go up to Iowa to reunite with the family. The Iowa Hawkeyes and the Minnesota Golden Gophers played football that weekend. It was a family tradition to go to the games and this year it was in Minneapolis.

It was going to be the first time seeing that series, so it was a great time to go and see the whole family after so many years.

My dad always planned the trip the weekend of that game be it in Iowa City or Minneapolis. He looked forward to it so much. Making plans for his family and friends gave him a lot of joy. He was very kind, a 6 foot 4-inch tall gentle giant. He was the travel agent for the weekend of that game. He was loved by so many and the best dad. I heard a story about him once, you see he drove the school bus, and the kids called him, "Bob the bus driver." They absolutely loved him. He apparently would let a dog or two on the bus so they wouldn't get run over, pretty cool. When he retired the next driver wouldn't let the dogs on and one was run over and killed. It was great seeing everyone again. I lost it when I saw my nieces and nephews. I broke down in tears for I didn't think I would ever see them again. They are special to me and all you have to do is read one of my children's books and you would understand.

13

BACK TO THE DESERT

After Thanksgiving I returned to Mesa. The last year or so I had been renting a room at a house in Mesa. It was a house turned into bedrooms with a common bathroom and common kitchen with a laundry room next to it. The washer and dryer were coin operated, so you always had to have some quarters fcol. There were seven tenants, each of whom had struggled with alcohol and other drugs. We all had our own problems. One of the rules was no drugs, so that was why I chose the place. Turned out it wasn't true. I could tell shortly thereafter that the land lady didn't give a shit. Most importantly there was nobody that did crack there when I was on probation.

I met a lot of interesting people at that house. Some were really cool, good people but others, not so much. One of the good ones was a dude that went by the nickname, Chief. He was playing guitar in his room one time, so I walked down the hall to check it out. That is where we became friends. Through Chief is how I met Kookie. I've always been drawn to Native Americans for some reason. Probably because they are awesome people. Chief is quite the guitar player he is really good. A request for Led Zeppelin or Van Halen? Yeah, that good.

I had been writing some poetry which, was something, new for me. One day we were hanging out and I asked him if he wanted to make some songs. Chief had many original songs that he came up with, but, didn't write lyrics. He would play one of his originals and I would look through my poetry trying to fit the words in with his music. Before you knew it, we made a total of 13 songs. Unfortunately, neither of us know how to write music and I can't play guitar like Chief. We named ourselves, "Black Algae Days". Chief is a pool cleaner so that is where the black algae comes from and one of my favorite songs ever is, "Black Days". So, Black Algae Days was born. Man, I can't stop laughing write now. We did a few gigs and people like our music. We were just having fun, but, were serious about the music. We had a message of advice for example the first song we wrote was, "Put It down down keep it down!" It was a song I wrote about putting down the crack pipe.

After probation was history a couple of crack heads move into the house. Thank God it was after probation, because the temptation was too much for me. I did relapse and smoked the rest of 2006. It was a nightmare all over again it seemed. The paranoia was real, always thinking if I get busted it's not going to be good. The thought that if I get caught I would surely do time didn't make me stop. I can't explain it just please don't try it.

The thing that made me stop is what happened that Christmas Eve. My sisters, in-laws, are snow birds, so they have a place and stay in the desert for the winter. My sister and her family always get together for Christmas dinner during the season. Her family was there and I was invited for Christmas Eve dinner. I had been smoking for about two months once again, so I was living in the disease. It almost makes me sick just thinking about it. We scored that morning and smoked all day. Driving with the stuff, just really bad judgement. It's incredibly sad what that crap will make you do. I can remember pulling into an apartment complex and me and some dude smoked a rock. I had a sun roof so we would blow the smoke through it. The thing is crack has a certain smell and the smoke seems different in some ways to me. Watching the road and the parking lot around you like a paranoid freak. Oh God please no cops anywhere please no cops. Thank God the Father for answering that prayer.

We made it back and it was time to get ready for Christmas Eve dinner with my sister and her family. I got myself together and made the thirty, minute drive to far East Mesa. Great seeing them they are a special family. My nieces omg are the best. I like to entertain the children and give them a hard time you know. I must, I'm the crazy uncle Dave.

I remember looking at one of them and I think she saw that something was wrong and she just looked at me with a concerned look. My smiles were off because I was sick once again. It made me feel rotten because, here I have time to spend time with them, but that bloody crack. I really hate it now! That was the moment I knew I had to stop because it's all about the children. The innocent children are relying on the adults for direction and, we, as adults have and are still failing. I started thinking about the things I learned in rehab and at the meetings, so, I used my "Tool box" and was able to stop and I have not smoked crack since. My poor Ophelia was suffering once I could see as well.

14

THE CLUB

By the beginning of January, 2007, I survived and fled the crack laden house and was able to stay with some guys I knew. It turned out that they were smoking meth, so I out of there and got my own place. Now it was time to find a job. I knew a friend of a friend that worked at a night club. By the end of January, I was working the parking lots a security guard, showing people where to park and collecting money since we worked for tips. At the end of the night we would pool the tips together and split the money.

The club was a hip-hop club and it could get a little rough at times. The patrons were mostly made up of drug dealers, gangster and other criminals. A small percentage of people that came to the club weren't from those groups and consisted of working class folks to professional athletes. There were a few fights to break up from time to time, and always had to be on the look for weapons. One night there were a few guys causing problems and they were taken out hard. Later after we closed for the night we walked the girls to their vehicles. I had gotten back to the front and was waiting for the door to open when a car came driving up to curb in front. I turned to look at what was going on, and then the passenger side window went down and I saw I guy with sun glasses looking out the window and he had a gun pointing at the doors. I fell to the ground and hid in front of a car. Then I started yelling, "Gun, gun, get down, get down." There were a few shots and then they sped away. The other guys then came running to the front with guns drawn. It happened so fast, I was just glad nobody got shot.

It was a tough job having to be on our feet for nine to ten hours. That was the worst part, because there was no sitting allowed. It's funny to think about, but the shoes were very important. There were also a lot of bad attitudes walking around, but you had to be cool, so you could get those tips. One night when I was working the front parking lot a car pulled up with some gangsters in it. They asked me if I wanted to make some extra cash selling coke. No way brother, I just told them I played with the lady in white and got burned. It was all cool they just laughed and drove away. Besides, I didn't sell drugs I just used them. Ultimately drugs ended up using me.

After about seven months I was promoted to bar-back. That meant more money and also more responsibility. The main thing for all of us was safety and security. Now, I got to take care of the bartenders and make sure they had everything the needed. They were great young ladies, hot and very good at what they did. There was a strict rule about dating the girls so I kept it professional. Actually, I was still dealing with the crack catastrophe in my head. I felt like a dirt bag and didn't think I was worth the love of a beautiful girl. I was my own worst critic, and enemy for that matter.

A few months went by and I was promoted to assistant manager. Once again, more money, but no where to go but down after that. All was going well, then I noticed a large lump on Ophelia's neck. I took her to the vet and it turned out to be cancerous. I convinced myself that it was because of my smoking crack and she got sick off the second-hand smoke, so I blamed myself. I had to put her down, so it was my fault she was gone. I killed her and wanted to kill myself. I was devastated beyond belief, utterly demolished. She was the only one that depended on me and cared about me. My selfish addiction killed her.

I fell deeper into depression. I lasted at the club a few more months and then one night the manager I was working with started doing heroin at the end of the night. That was enough for me, so after a year and a half, I just walked out and never looked back. I thank the Lord that I didn't get tempted to the point of trying it. That would surly would have been the end of me. Some of the stories I heard about that drug are terrifying.

I got to the point where my will to live was once again fading. I decided that sometime in the future I was going to kill myself. The plan was if the world didn't end on 12/21/12 I would go down to the Gulf-of-Mexico, walk out into the ocean and be gone.

15

THE NETHERLANDS

I grew to hate the desert. It disgusted me. In 2010, at the end of May, I left Arizona. Social media reunited me with a friend I grew up with in Alton, IL. He had moved to Utrecht, a city in the Netherlands. We were messaging and I told him I was going to move. I just knew somewhere in the Midwest because my dad had Parkinson's disease and I wanted to be closer to him. Jake, told me that his family moved to Kansas City, MO years ago, and mentioned to get a hold of his brother Blake.

As Jake and I were talking the idea of living in the Netherlands for the summer came up. A plan was beginning to take shape. First, I would drive to Kansas City and leave my SUV with Blake as I went to live in Europe for the summer. All I wanted to do was leave the desert and now that was going to happen.

The Eyjafjallajokull volcano, located in Iceland erupted in April, don't ask me how to pronounce its name. The eruption actually halted travel to Europe due to the ash cloud for about a month, so I wasn't sure if the trip was going to happen. They deemed it safe to fly a couple of weeks before my flight, so the first thing was to drive to Kansas City.

I reunited with my friend Jake, spent a few days in KC and then it was off to the Netherlands.

My itinerary was to fly to Chicago from KC, then catch a connecting flight to Stockholm, Sweden, then fly to Dusseldorf, Germany and finally catch the train to Utrecht. I was a bit anxious not ever being to Europe before, but I was ready for an adventure.

When I arrived in Germany it was time to catch the train to Utrecht. I was on a schedule, so I had about an hour to get where I need to go to catch the bullet train to Holland. I'm part German, but I don't speak the language except basic words like hello and thank you. A bit in a panic I found some police officers and tried to get some help. Europeans speak at least four languages and everyone speaks English. They played dumb and acted like they didn't know any English, so I moved on. I found the small train station, but there was nothing about specific train rides to a certain city. The trains were all headed east and I needed to go west, so I was getting a bit concerned. I finally asked an older gentleman what I should do, and he motioned to me to board the train going east, and about 10 or so kilometers east there was a station with connecting train rides. He was a friendly older German man, like a grandpa, and he was with his grandchildren it seemed. I listened to him and boarded the train with him and his family and off I went.

Sure enough, about ten minutes later we got to the large station. I was relieved and thank the gentleman and his family for it seemed five minutes or so. At the end we were all laughing and I felt safe once again. I found the connecting train, boarded and a few minutes later we sped off to Utrecht. I was so relieved and able to relax and enjoy the ride. A cool thing is they serve beer on the trains, so I got a brew and settled in my seat with a smile on my face.

A couple of hours later we arrived at the train station in Utrecht. My buddy Blake was going to meet in the station somewhere, so I started walking through the station and looking for my childhood friend. It was interesting checking out all the people and then I realized I needed a bathroom soon. When I found one to my surprise is you had to pay to use the toilet. Oh boy, I need to get some coins and quickly. Got the coins and I avoided a situation they could have been a bit messy.

Now, it was time to find Blake and his girlfriend. A few minutes later we found one another and off to his apartment we went. Blake had a nice crib. It was on the second floor with a balcony and a sweet view.

We cracked open a Heineken and toasted each other since it was the first we had seen each other in many years.

If you didn't know, pot and prostitution are legal in the Netherlands. We finished the Heineken and then it was off to a coffee shop to get high. Besides pot, hash was also legal. Those were the only two drugs legal to buy. The whole time in Holland, not one time did I witness anyone doing or anybody offered me cocaine, crack, heroin or meth. Also, hard liquor wasn't around because everyone just drank beer and smoked weed if they wanted. Sure, you could order a drink at a bar, but it wasn't common. I have to tell you it was awesome not having hard liquor or hard drugs around.

It's a smart system they have in Holland, and the coffee shops are interesting places. First, there is no alcohol allowed, and actually illegal to sell beer or whatever in one. They served coffee, juice, soda pop etc. Also, they sold snacks like pastries and other goodies, well of course people are smoking pot. There were many people with the munchies, laughing and having conversations. People weren't angry, drunk or violent they were just having a good relaxing time. You could have 5 grams or less in your possession, anymore it was illegal, and you would be considered a drug dealer. When people were done doing their thing they would give thanks and be on their way, folks were real chill.

My drug of choice is reefer, so living in place where that, hash and prostitution are legal was a bit like paradise to me. Saying that I did isolate myself, because I really just wanted to be alone and smoke weed and have meaningless sex. I had a plan and this was going to be my last hurrah you could say.

It was a great summer, we had a lot of fun and it was a summer when the World Cup was played. I think it's safe to say everyone knows that soccer is huge in Europe not to mention Holland. The Netherlands had a great team that year, so it was a great atmosphere and a lot of hope to win the Cup.

There was a bar across the street from the apartment, so we would go there to watch the games. The bar was called, "Arno's", and yes say it like a pirate. It was so much fun watching the games there it was a huge party every time. The color of Holland is bright orange and blue. In the bars or on the streets all you saw on game day was orange. It was quite the atmosphere.

Arno was quite the character. He was around six feet tall with curly blond hair and robust. He just reminded me of a pirate. We became good friends to the point we would be rough with each other kind of like how pirates act towards each other. There were orange plastic blow horns you could buy to blow in celebration when a goal was scored or just if you wanted to be a bit crazy and have fun. A few times during a celebration after a score sometimes we would hit each other on the head with the horns, grunt like a pirate and then have a Heineken and cheer on the Orange Lion which was what they called the soccer team.

On the days when there wasn't a soccer match, I would do some hiking through out the city. Grab a back pack with some water, snacks and a blanket, oh yeah weed and beer as well. When I had all my stuff together, I would be on my way to explore and enjoy Utrecht and the country side. It was so cool discovering a park, sitting down and smoking a joint just chilling and not wanting to cause any problems, just enjoying the day.

We also joined a gym and worked out every day. The gym had some kayaks you could sign out and cruise the canals, it was great. That's one of the cool things about Holland there are many canals throughout the country. Kayaking the canals in the city was awesome. Checking out the architecture, the people sitting at the outdoor cafes next to the canals and the trees. It was so beautiful and something I will never forget. One time as we were kayaking we come upon what is called, "The boats". I soon found out that the boats were a legal, floating prostitution store. It was like a strip mall and all the shops were selling sex. My head kind of exploded, it was mind blowing. I found out how to get there when I went hiking one day, so I did check the mall out a few times.

At night we would go to the bars and night clubs and drink beer. Holland is located so for north that the days would last until about midnight in the summer. Around five hours of darkness, so that was wild. Bikes were everywhere and there would be group rides all night so you had to watch where you were walking or a heard of bikes would run you down. It was different seeing so many bikes and so few cars. Not many people owned one because they all road bikes, walked and took the trains to get where they were going. Actually, it was nice having few cars driving around because you could breath clean air.

I went to a couple of concerts that summer, and they were adventurous as well. Alice In Chains were playing in Eindhoven one night so I took the train the morning of the show to the city. I didn't have tickets to the show because it was sold out, so I wasn't sure if was even going to see them. I got a hotel room so no matter what I was staying the night in Eindhoven. . Beautiful little city Eindhoven is and smartly laid out as well. The train station is on the edge of town. Once exiting the station to the left was the concert hall about half a kilometer. To the right was the entrance to the town. After I check into the hotel I walked the streets of Eindhoven to look for a coffee house. I score my weed and then back to the hotel to chill before I went to the venue and try to scalp a ticket. It was awesome because as I was getting close to it this dude saw me walked towards me then asked if I needed a ticket. We made the transaction and then back to the hotel to get ready. I found a bar on the way and stopped in for a few Heinekens. cool visiting with the people, they are great. After getting a good buzz on it was time to go to AIC. I've seen them a few times and it was another awesome show. After the show a few more beers, then back to the room and in the morning, it was back to Utrecht.

The second concert I saw in Holland was The Cult. Sonic Temple was my first CD I ever purchased when I live in El Paso. The show was in Den Hague. Before I went to the concerts I looked at maps of the cities.

Eindhoven was easy to find like I wrote, but the hall in Den Hague wasn't. The map showed it was about a five kilometer walk southeast of the train station. The Hague was a lot bigger city the Eindhoven. I didn't see any taxis, so I started walking northwest when I left the station. At first, I couldn't find it, but after about three hours I did. I was getting frustrated since I couldn't find the place, and the show was going to start in about and hour. As I was walking I came up to another street I took a right and about two blocks down, was, what looked like a tour bus. As I ran past the bus there was a building on the right and got to the front of the building I looked up and there was the name of the venue. I noticed the dude from Eindhoven that I got the AIC ticket and bam he had one for The Cult. Another great show, and on the walk to the show, I didn't notice any hotels, so I walked back to the station and went back to Eindhoven. There was about two weeks left until I flew back to Kansas City, so the party was on.

16

MELISSA AND NICOLE

I flew back to Kansas City at the end of August. Summer was over so, as far as I was concerned it was one of my last ones. Spending the summer in the Netherlands was great, and then reality set in. Was this my last summer? A couple of weeks into September I decided to put the plan in motion. Basically, live, go home and then off to Texas to take a swim until I couldn't anymore.

I convinced myself that some good would come out of this. I've always wanted to help my parents, and that was the mindset I had, when I'm gone they could have all I had left which would have helped them. Since life was coming to and end for me I started drinking heavily again and smoked weed when friends would come around.

December had arrived, and I was going to see my family at Christmas, so I was anxious. It was December 3rd now, and it was my nieces, birthday. She was a blessing God gave to my sister and brother-in-law. Just an awesome young lady who has become an awesome young woman. Some time that day I called her, and we chatted for a bit. What a joy she has been.

The next day was the 4th of December and the started out like any other day. Get up, get stoned and get things ready for the plan I had. Sometime during the day, I got a phone call from a friend that lived in Phoenix, Hillbilly. The news wasn't good instead it was heartbreaking. To of the girls, bartenders, that worked with at the club were found murdered that morning. Turns out the murders happened some time the night before, they were strangled to death. To this day there still has been no arrests or suspects.

What I read was nobody had heard from them for a while. A friend of theirs and another bartender went over to the house where they were living to check up on them. When she got to the front door it was locked, and their cars were in the driveway. She rang the doorbell and knocked, but there was no answer. Then, she went around back to the deck to see if they might be smoking a cigarette. They weren't there, then she looked in the window, and she saw a lifeless body on the floor.

She called 911 after the horrendous discovery, and, waited for the police. When they got there broke down the door and confirmed that both Nicole and Melissa were murdered. They found Nicole in the kitchen and Melissa in one of the bedrooms. The door being locked, and no forced entry tells me that they probably knew the people. They later found out that Melissa was eight weeks pregnant, so those people murdered three people one being an unborn baby.

I couldn't believe what I was hearing. Two beautiful young women who I worked with and became my friends were found murdered. I'm know that Melissa had a crush on me, so that tore me apart. Maybe if I would have gone out with her a relationship could have formed, and I could have gotten her away from that club. It confirmed my thinking, I screwed up again and two young women, were murdered. I felt a bit responsible in a way, so I was ready to end my life.

Nicole Glass was a blond hair blue eyed little fire cracker. She was so spunky and always smiling. I can still hear the words she said to me one night. Something happened, and I helped her with it and when we were done she said, "Dave you are spicy". I just laughed and told her the same thing.

Melissa was Persian and Hispanic. She was a beautiful brown eyed senorita. I couldn't see how a beautiful young woman like Melissa would ever want anything to do with me. She was twenty-five with her whole life ahead of her and I was a forty-three-year old piece of crap. That's how I felt about myself. I didn't want to get close to anyone or I would probably ruin, there, life as well. One night when I was working I got a pitcher of soda from her. She gave it to me with this cute smile on her face. I am a little shy, I was a shy guy, and when I looked into her eyes a freaked out a bit and couldn't think of anything, so I turned and went on my way. I think of that moment in time always and get upset with myself to this day.

I didn't know how something so terrible could happen to two lovely ladies. There are some shady folks hanging out at club, and someone talked Nicole into something illegal. There were many arrests and people think it was a hit on her to silence her. Melissa was in the wrong place at the wrong time. There has still been no arrest, so please pray for them and their families for justice.

17

GRACE

December 22nd, I left for Waukon, IA, to spend Christmas with the family before I left for Texas. I was distraught and depressed because what had happened to my two friends in Phoenix a few weeks earlier.

I was so ready to execute the plan and end my life, because I felt as if I failed again and lost my will to live. I didn't deserve to live, I didn't deserve to be loved, I deserved to die. It was time to check-out.

The next day was December 23rd and I was still upset. Many emotions were flowing through me. The night I went to one of the restaurants in town and took a seat at the bar. I had one too many beers by the time I left the bar. When I walked outside it had started to snow at a pretty good clip. The roads were already in bad shape with much of them covered in ice, and now they were snow covered. It had probably snowed about six inches by then. I was thinking to myself that I needed to be careful driving back to the house. Since I was convicted of a DUI back in 2005 because of my crack addiction another, DUI, wouldn't be good. If I got another one, I'd probably go to jail, and that wasn't a part of my plan.

I wasn't feeling good about driving still thinking about what happened five and a half years ago. I got into the SUV and decided to take the back-way home around the golf course. The road goes up a hill and then there's a big curve to the left. As I was turning to follow the bend I fishtailed and slipped into the ditch. There are few houses along the road, but it was about midnight, so they were dark, and everyone was probably asleep.

I opened the door, jumped out and the snow in the ditch was probably up to my chest. I started freaking out because I didn't know what to do. I was just hoping I didn't wake someone because they would call the cops. I knew that I was over the legal limit when came to, driving, so I thought my goose was cooked. I tried to push the SUV back and it might have worked if it was in neutral and not park. My mind was racing. I was a half mile from the house, so I decide to walk home and figure things out from there. I left the lights on, so they were shining bright and I was afraid it would cause some attention.

When I got to the house I was panicking a little bit. What was I going to do? Waukon is a sleepy little town and I didn't know anyone with a truck. My dad was dying from Parkinson's disease, so there was nothing they could do. As I paced the floor a though came to my mind. Get on the computer and search for a tow truck. Just maybe there would be one and they were awake.

The first place I found, immediately I called the number, but there was no answer. The second place I called I got a recording that said they were done for the night. There was one more number to try, so hope was fading. I called expecting no response, but after a couple of rings somebody answered. I had a glimmer of hope that things might just work out. I gave him my address and he said he'd be there in ten minutes. When he got to the house, I jumped in and off we went to the place that my SUV was stuck. Many thoughts were going through my head. Surely someone had called the police, and there was going to be someone at the scene. Was I going to be arrested for another DUI? Was I going to lose my freedom once again? I was expecting the worst and hoping for the best.

In the distance we could see the bright lights of the SUV, but there were no police lights flashing. We got to it and there wasn't anyone around, no one. He put the chain on the back and a couple of seconds later I was loose. He followed me to the house upon request just in case another ditch was in my future. I pulled into the driveway and I was shaking thinking about what could have been and because how it all turned out. I ran into the house and got some money. I came back out and asked him how much it was going to be, and I think he said twenty dollars. I smiled, gave him sixty or so dollars and gave him a hug thanking him for a few minutes. I shook his hand and went back in the house in disbelief. When I got inside I fell to my knees and sobbed thinking how it could have turned out. Thank you, Lord, and my God.

18

A RADIANT LIGHT

When I woke up the next morning, Christmas Eve, I told my parents about the events of the night before. They were disappointed, but happy it all turned out well. My dad gave me forty dollars being the kind man he was. I accepted it and gave him a hug.

As the day went by I was still shook up and in shock about what happened the previous night. Also, I was still grieving because of the murders of Melissa and Nicole in Phoenix. Midday, I had a talk with my mom and told her that I thought it would be better if I would die, because then they could have what I had left. She said no, but I was still going to go on with my plan of suicide. I was at the end of my rope and I was going to let go.

The family got together for Christmas Eve dinner later in the day at my, sisters home. It was great spending time with everyone especially my nieces. There little faces so full of love and life. My youngest niece was still a believer in Santa Claus. That afternoon I was talking to her about Christmas and Santa. She told me about the "Elf on the shelf". I had heard of the game, but, didn't know what it was all about. She seriously told me that each night until Christmas day, the elf would move from one place to another. I questioned her about it and said, "That is really cool, but are you really sure about the elf moving from one place to other?" She looked at me with a convincingly and said, "Oh yes, my friend stayed over the other night and we heard bells!" I smiled, chuckled, turn away from and shed a tear. I love children they are the best, so innocent. I thought to myself, "Why is the world so evil and why do the children have to grow up?"

We all decided to go to midnight mass that evening. When night fell we went to St. Patrick's Catholic Church for mass. It was a packed house when we got there, and the pews were quite full. There was no way that we could all sit together, so I told them I would just sit in the back row and for them to find a spot where they could all sit together. I kept my eyes closed and head bowed during mass and just listened. Thinking about what happened the night before, my nieces and the plan that I had to kill myself, I started to cry. During the readings of the Scriptures and Gospel, my tears continued coming more heavily.

Father Joseph Schneider was the priest at the time for St. Patrick's. After the Gospel reading there is a homily from the priest. I was listening intently, and tears continued falling with my eyes firmly closed. The homily was about forgiveness and hope.

Father Joe started talking about sin and how we all sin, even himself. I was balling at that point and then he said, "Accept Gods forgiveness for you sins and become a beacon of hope for other's". He said those words over and over, and it seemed like he said it one hundred times. I was still crying with my eyes closed and all-of-a sudden it seemed like he was talking right in my ear. The voice I heard got my attention and I thought to myself, "What's going on? He has said those words for a while now."

Then, I lifted my head up and I could feel the tears running down my cheeks, opened my eyes and look at Father Joe. I was a bit startled because it seemed like he was looking right at me, and then I noticed his piercing eyes that were looking right through me. It seemed like we were face, to face, and then he was back in the same place he was when I first opened my eyes. Then I noticed a light shining from above on to Father Joe.

The light was so bright it was radiant. He looked like he was glowing. Rays of light were shooting out and up from him. As I followed the cylindrical radiant light back up to the ceiling there seemed to be silver and gold particles floating in the light. My eyes were wide open now and my jaw dropped to the floor. There was a shadow deep in the light and I was startled again. Then a smile fell over my face and a felt a powerful energy rush through me. It hard to explain, but it was a feeling of joy. All the negative thoughts and feeling had left me. Committing suicide was the farthest thing I was thinking about in my mind, some, how, I felt changed. I looked around in amazement then the light was gone. I had no idea what I had witnessed, but it was a beautiful, radiant light that was breath-taking.

19

REBORN

After seeing the light, I was changed. The shame, despair and guilt I felt from leaving the school where I taught, to buy crack, was gone. It felt like a huge weight had been lifter from my shoulders. I felt joyous! I felt I was loved the first time in a long time. It's difficult to explain.

After the arrest I started to write. The words were rushing into my mind so fast I couldn't write it all down. There was a poem/story I wrote a few days after the arrest and it was titled, "A Day at The Park with Friends." Here it is:

A Day at The Park with Friends

Josh, Amelia, Sydney, Fifi, Sassy and Sky went for a walk one day
and they looked for a park to play.
When they finally found one oh boy did they have fun
There were slides there were swings
They glided as if they had wings
They had so much fun playing in the sun
Going round and round up and down
When they were done having so much fun

Some thugs came to them they had some drugs
The friends looked each other in the eye
They remember what their uncle said
Try drugs and you'll be dead
Uncle said he loves us very much and doesn't want us to do that stuff
Don't be influenced by someone bad he said this because he had
He said, "Scream and run away!" Then go tell mom and dad
They would be very proud they would be glad
Now when the friends go to the park they know how to react
If someone offers them marijuana, heroin, meth, cocaine and crack

When I got back to Kansas City after Christmas I started going to church every day in the morning. I was longing to figure out what I had seen and why I felt so different. One day I was thinking about the line, scream and run away. I felt like that could scare children, so it had to be something different. I was thinking about the line one afternoon and the words and vision, Yell No! Let's Go! came to my mind. That was it, yell no let's go. Also, the name Christopher kept coming to my mind. Christopher is the name my grandma Butler suggested for my birth name, so I decided to make my penname for the children's books, Christopher David.

The last four months of 2010, my parents kept telling me about a girl named Jenn and that I should give her a call. She was a friend of one of my, moms, friends. Now, I had a plan that after Christmas I was going to Texas and walk into the ocean never to be seen again. I wanted nothing to do with her or anybody for that matter, because I was going to be dead in a matter of months.

After seeing the light that all changed, and I decided to give her a call because she struggled with depression. I knew I had to try to help her any way I could. Well, after calling her a few times I left a message explaining who I was and wondered if she wanted to get together some time to meet. I left my cell number and hung up the phone.

A week or two passed and had not gotten any response from Jenn, so I figured she wasn't interested. I kept going to church wondering what I had witnessed. One evening my mom called me and said to expect a call from Jenn. It turned out she got my message, but lost the number, so she called their mutual friend and got it again.

Another couple of weeks passed and then I got the call from Jennifer. We talked for a while a decided to meet the upcoming weekend for a burger and karaoke in Westport. She had gone through a rough stretch which something I could understand. We met and we both had a good time, so we kept in touch and became friends. I hadn't heard from her for a while and then she called me from a hospital. She was struggling with life and asked if I could come visit her. I took her a little stuffed lamb and some candy that she asked for. She was going to be discharged the day of a concert I was going to, so I got her a ticket and we went to see, Three Days Grace.

One day we were hanging out and I told her what I had witnessed. Jennifer grew up, Baptist, but converted to Catholicism a few years before I met her. She was very knowledgeable of the bible, and I was a cradle Catholic, so I wasn't. She had many bibles and I didn't have one, so she gave me one to read. She showed me the story of Saul, who I had never heard of. I read it and I learned that he wasn't the nicest person at the time, and he saw a bright light as well. I was surprised because something like that had just happened to me. Then Jennifer said to me, "Do you know what you saw?" I said, "Was it Jesus?" Then she replied, "No, you've seen the light of the Holy Spirit." After that things were making more sense to me and clarity came to me, so I was more understanding, of what I had witnessed, the light of the Holy Spirit. I've got good news people, the Father, the Son and the Holy Spirit are real!

EPILOGUE

You don't want your children to become addicted to drugs as I did, it is horrible a living hell. I want all children out there to understand that doing drugs is utterly wrong and not cool. Drugs are evil, and only send you down a road to nowhere. Drugs kill, if they don't kill you, they will- kill, your dreams. Yes, I survived my addiction, but I should have died at least one hundred times. I know I've done a lot of damage to myself and will die earlier than I should have.

If you are using drugs and like the feeling, then you are addicted. Believe me those euphoric feeling will turn to misery at some point, and then you'll be in trouble. Ask for help before it's to late and you end up in jail or die of an overdose. You will find strength is asking for help. The only one you are fooling is yourself.

If you know of a family member that is struggling with addiction have the courage to get them help, because they absolutely need you love, support and empathy. The cocaine and crack addiction that I lived through were the most horrifically terrifying, and despair filled circumstances I have ever experienced. It's not something I would wish on my worst enemy. You are love so much, and have too much love to give, so don't waste your life on drugs. It took me many years, but I have accepted, Gods forgiveness for my sins, so I have forgiven myself. Gods love has truly saved me, and Gods love will save you as well.

Jennifer and my friendship turned into something more than we both ever expected, and we moved in together. On August 8th, 2012 Jenn and I were married in Waukon, at St. Patrick's by Father Joe. I started the process of trademarking YELL NO! LET'S GO! in 2011 and secured the mark in 2012, then started the children's book project. I've published three such books, "A Day At The Park With Friends", "A Day At The Zoo With Friends", and "A Day At The Bowling Alley With Friends". They are available through Xlibris Publishing or my website @ yellnoletsgo.com.

Since I've witnessed the light of the Holy Spirit, I've seen some amazing things as well. For instance, I have been outside on a sunny day, and it will get so bright that I'm blinded to the point of only seeing a foot in front of me and I had to feel my way inside then my sight comes back.

Another time I was out front, and something told me to go to the back yard. We have a car port on the right side of the house with a SUV under it. I walked around it slowly to take-a-look in the back yard to see if something was going on. My favorite bird is the Cardinal and to my amazement when I peaked in the back it was littered with cardinals. They filled the yard there were hundreds of male cardinals, but there were none in the other yards. It was amazing what I was seeing. I wasn't sure if I was really seeing what I thought, so I walked to back and when I got to the fence the sea of red on the ground became a sea of red in the air, as they took flight. I just stood there in wonder. It was amazing.

One more story I'd like to tell you is one evening after dinner, jenn and I were sitting on the bench in the front of the house. I looked to my left for some reason, and notices what looked to be a cat crouching down on the other side of the car kind of peering out. I told Jenn to look at this cat I was seeing, and, called out to it. I got its attention and it got up and walked around the car. To our amazement the cat looked like a little bobcat as it walked slowly towards us. It was a golden, brown color and at least a yard long. As it approached us I was hoping this large cat, that looked like a bobcat, wasn't going to attack us or something. It got to my leg and rubbed against me then it lifted itself and gently bumped my leg with its head. We stood up and I picked it up under the front legs and gave it a kiss on the top of its head. I put the gentle little bobcat back down and turned to Jenn. We smiled at each other and kissed then we looked back down, and the littler bobcat was gone. We looked under the cars, in the back yard and walked around looking everywhere for it, but no little bobcat. To this day we have still not seen it again.

About three days later Jenn got a notification on her phone from a no kill shelter in the area. They had just gotten a little pastel calico kitty. We went to check it out, because we wanted another cat since Jenn's Persian cat Buddy had since passed away. The kitty's name was Juliet and it was a golden brown, color, with light black patches. First, she reached out the kennel for Jennifer. I was sitting looking at the sweet little kitty, and when they let it out of the kennel she walked over to me and rubbed against my leg as she raised her self and gave a bump. I thought about the little bobcat the other day and knew Juliet was a gift from above. Juliet acts so much like my calico cat Ophelia who passed away in 2008. Is it a coincidence? I don't think so, for there are no such thing as coincidences. These are just a few of the amazing things that have happened since seeing the light.

Now, this is where the story gets even more unbelievable. It turned out that Jenn was engaged to be engaged a handful of years before I met her. Her boyfriend was the son of Jenn's and my mom's mutual friend. His name was Alex and we are both from the same small town in Iowa. Alex was seven years younger than me, so I didn't know him or his family. Also, I didn't know about the tragedy that happened three and a half years earlier in 2007. Alex was an addict like me. He became addicted to alcohol and opioids and died of an accidental opioid overdose in the fall of 2007. He was probably one of the first to succumb to the opioid epidemic. He was a great dude I hear, and most addicts are the nicest people, we just made a mistake and tried drugs. Learn from me and remember when there's bullying, danger, drugs or violence…Yell No! Let's Go!

yellnoletsgo.com
yellnoletsgo.net

Printed in the United States
Baker & Taylor Publisher Services